Dealing with Loss - A Workbook for Kids
(Edition 2)

Author: Stacey Hughes

Copyright

Dealing with Loss - A Workbook for Kids (Edition 2)

Copyright © 2013 by Stacey Hughes

All rights reserved. No part of this publication may be reproduced, distributed, or transmitted in any form or by any means, including photocopying, recording, or other electronic or mechanical methods, without the prior written permission of the author, except in the case of brief quotations embodied in critical reviews and certain other non-commercial uses permitted by copyright law. For permission requests, contact the author staceylhughes@hotmail.com

Imaginary Press
Lulu Press, Inc
www.lulu.com

Ordering Information:
Quantity sales. Special discounts are available on quantity purchases by corporations, associations and others. For details, contact the author at the email above

Printed in the United Kingdom

ISBN 978-1-291-42836-0
90000

For
Luke, Holly & Lachlan

Acknowledgements

I would like to thank my parents, my friends and the very special ladies of WTT

This book was created by Stacey Hughes

Stacey is a middle school teacher who worked in a number of schools over a ten year period before becoming a first time mum.

Her son, Luke, died of sudden infant death when he was just five days old. Luke had a congenital heart condition diagnosed shortly after birth and she learnt that despite babies being perfect on the outside, ultimately it was what was happening on the inside that mattered.

When Stacey lost her son she learnt that as a society we are not very good at dealing with grief. We don't know what to say or what to do and we find grieving and dealing with our feelings incredibly hard.

Stacey found enormous support from other bereaved parents and has since dedicated her time to improve support services for bereaved families.

She has since retrained in counselling and works extensively with bereaved families. But it was after the birth of her subsequent two children that Stacey recognised a need for practical resources.

Whilst Stacey's children did not meet their brother, they will forever live in a bereaved family. They will grow up knowing their brother has died and they may need help and support to deal with this throughout their lives.

And so this workbook was created. Combining her teaching skills and her experience of bereavement, Stacey has managed to create a hands on support that can be completed and revisited as required. It can be used in school, at home or both

Someone I love Isn't Here & I Really Miss Them

What is this book all about?

'Dealing with Loss - A Workbook for Kids'. This workbook enables kids to express themselves and their thoughts and feelings surrounding their loss. It can be used for a number of losses including bereavement.

The concept is for the child to personalise the book. To draw pictures, to write in, to scrawl, to add stickers and photographs and to make this book their own.

As adults we can find it difficult to ask questions and we generally struggle with knowing what questions to ask. This workbook is designed to help adults ask the right questions and to give you confidence when working with children.

Dealing with loss is very tricky, very emotional and lots of hard work. There is no right or wrong way to deal with loss and sadly there is no magic potion or powder to make the process any easier or quicker but with lots of support we can all learn to rebuild our lives.

This book belongs to...

I'd like to tell you about me...

- My name

- My age

- Where I live

- Who I live with

- My Hair Colour

- The Colour of My Eyes

- My Height

- My Birthday

- My Favourite Colour

- My Favourite Food

- My Favourite Sport

- My Pet

- My School

Here is a picture of me

This is where I live...

I live in

I live with

I'd like to draw a picture of my house

I'd like to tell you all about my family

This is My Family Tree

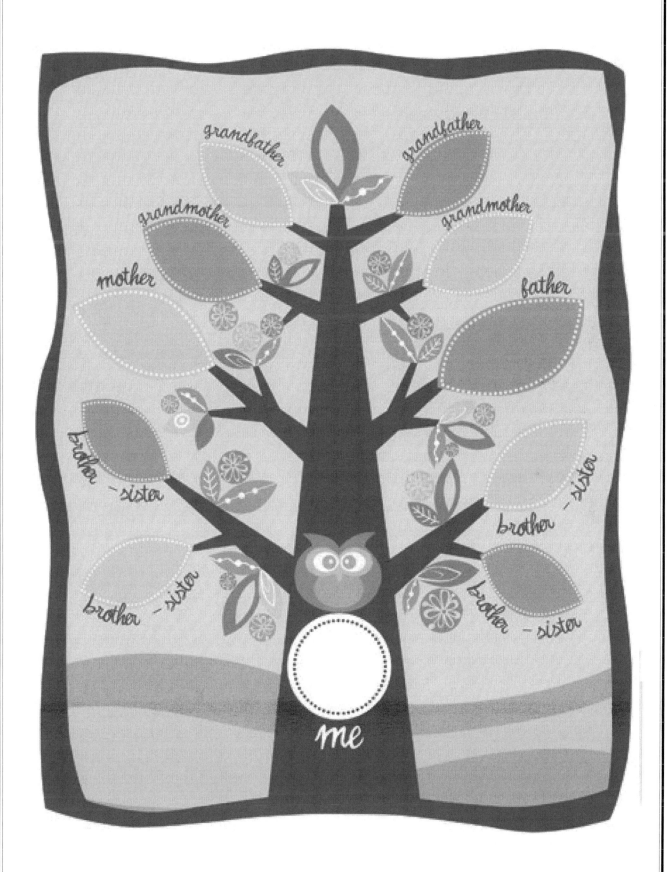

These are the things I like to do...

<u>In School</u>

<u>At Home</u>

I would like to tell you about my school

- <u>My School</u>

- <u>My Teacher</u>

- <u>My Class</u>

- <u>My Friends</u>

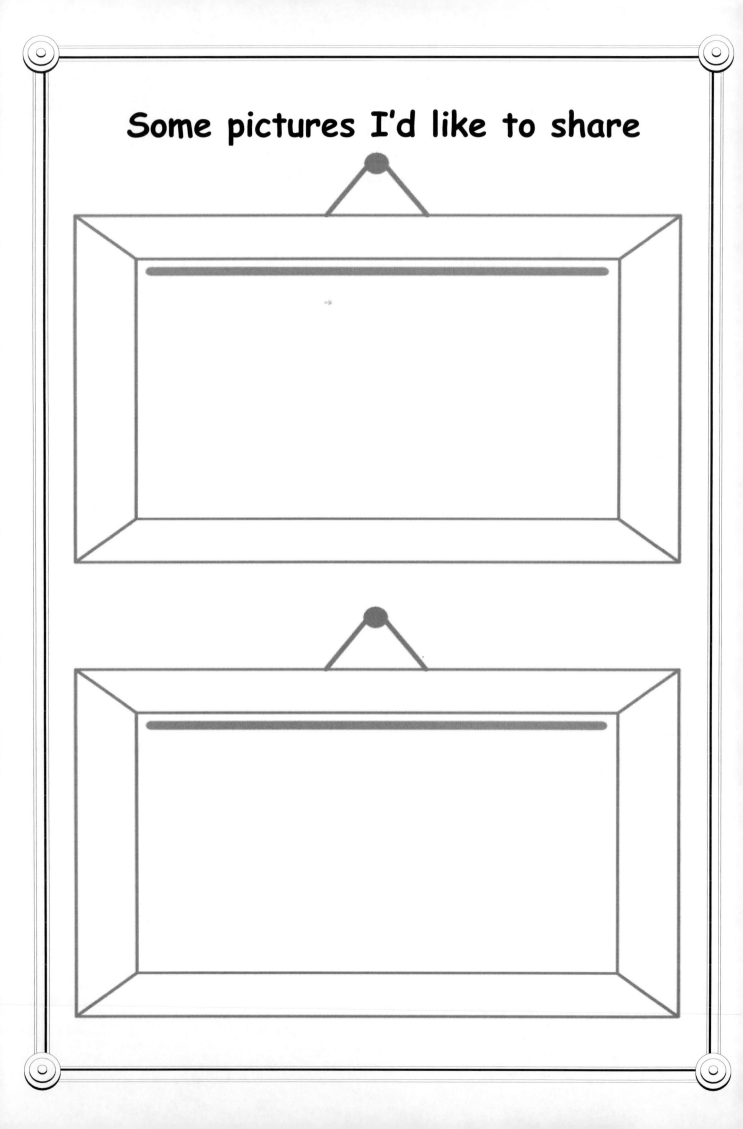

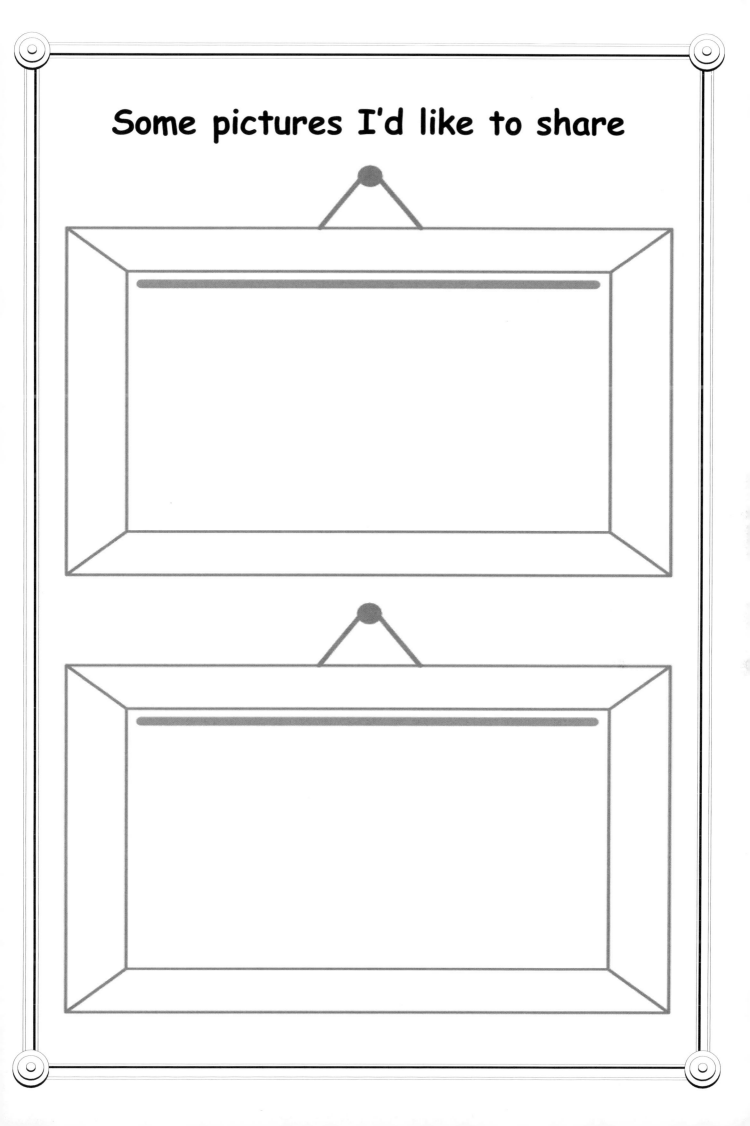

The person I miss is my...

_____

I'd like to tell you about them...

- Name

- Age

- Hair Colour

- Colour of Eyes

- Birthday

- Favourite Colour

- Favourite Food

- Favourite Sport

- Favourite Holiday

- School / Job

Here is a photograph

I'd like to tell you what happened to them

I remember lots of things about that day

And the days, weeks and months that followed

Some people say silly things to me, others say very nice things.

Word search

```
P U Y L D N D D A C
F Q L S E D E A N Y
H M L S T E S S G N
Y G I O I V U O R H
P P S R C O F L Y Q
Q J P C X L N O U P
O Q R A E F O N P J
S A F E H P C E S Y
Y P P A H N E L E J
S C A R E D U Y T Y
```

ANGRY   CONFUSED
CROSS   EXCITED
HAPPY   LONELY
LOVED   SAD
SAFE   SCARED
SILLY   UNHAPPY
UPSET

 I know when I am sad because

I know when I am angry because

 And I know when I am happy because

Sometimes I am happy
Sometimes I am sad

I am happy when...

I am sad when...

Things I can do to help me when I am sad

I have questions I'd like to ask. Some might sound really silly...

I'm scared of...

Stages of grief
The five stages of death and grief

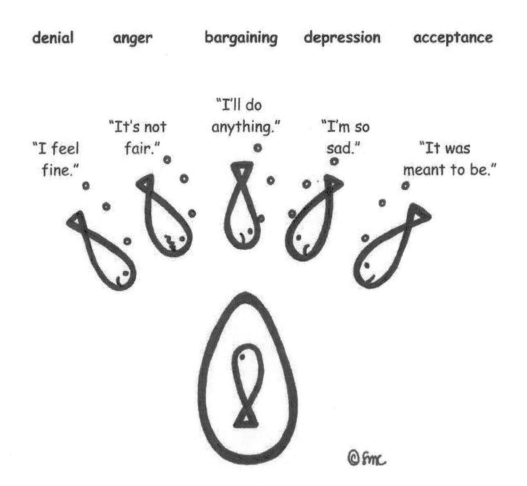

It is important to learn how to adapt to our new life after loss. Acceptance doesn't mean we have forgotten or that we don't hurt any more. It simply means we have learnt how to cope and manage our feelings better. We can still have sad and angry days but we have good days again too.

My Life, My Timeline

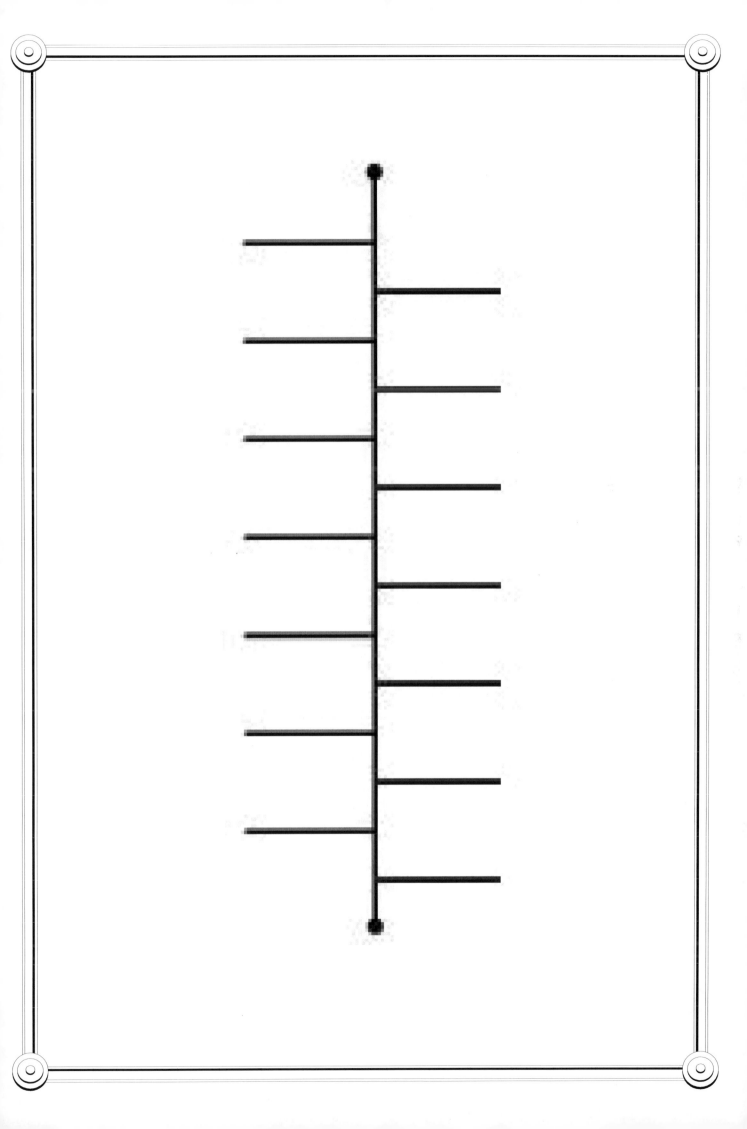

Life wasn't always perfect, but that doesn't mean we didn't love each other

I have lots of wonderful memories of you...

Memories

Memories

Poems

If I could have a lifetime wish
a dream that would come true
I'd pray to God with all my heart
for yesterday and you
A thousand words can't bring you back
I know because I've tried
And neither would a million tears
I know because I've cried
You left behind a broken heart
and happy memories too
I never wanted memories
I only wanted you.

You've just walked on ahead of me
And I've got to understand
You must release the ones you love
And let go of their hand.
I try and cope the best I can
But I'm missing you so much
If I could only see you
And once more feel your touch.
Yes, you've just walked on ahead of me
Don't worry I'll be fine
But now and then I swear I feel
Your hand slip into mine

A Poem I like
& A Poem by Me...

Certain dates can be hard

January
Mo	Tu	We	Th	Fr	Sa	Su
	1	2	3	4	5	6
7	8	9	10	11	12	13
14	15	16	17	18	19	20
21	22	23	24	25	26	27
28	29	30	31			

February
Mo	Tu	We	Th	Fr	Sa	Su
				1	2	3
4	5	6	7	8	9	10
11	12	13	14	15	16	17
18	19	20	21	22	23	24
25	26	27	28	29		

March
Mo	Tu	We	Th	Fr	Sa	Su
					1	2
3	4	5	6	7	8	9
10	11	12	13	14	15	16
17	18	19	20	21	22	23
24	25	26	27	28	29	30
31						

April
Mo	Tu	We	Th	Fr	Sa	Su
	1	2	3	4	5	6
7	8	9	10	11	12	13
14	15	16	17	18	19	20
21	22	23	24	25	26	27
28	29	30				

May
Mo	Tu	We	Th	Fr	Sa	Su
			1	2	3	4
5	6	7	8	9	10	11
12	13	14	15	16	17	18
19	20	21	22	23	24	25
26	27	28	29	30	31	

June
Mo	Tu	We	Th	Fr	Sa	Su
						1
2	3	4	5	6	7	8
9	10	11	12	13	14	15
16	17	18	19	20	21	22
23	24	25	26	27	28	29
30						

July
Mo	Tu	We	Th	Fr	Sa	Su
	1	2	3	4	5	6
7	8	9	10	11	12	13
14	15	16	17	18	19	20
21	22	23	24	25	26	27
28	29	30	31			

August
Mo	Tu	We	Th	Fr	Sa	Su
				1	2	3
4	5	6	7	8	9	10
11	12	13	14	15	16	17
18	19	20	21	22	23	24
25	26	27	28	29	30	31

September
Mo	Tu	We	Th	Fr	Sa	Su
1	2	3	4	5	6	7
8	9	10	11	12	13	14
15	16	17	18	19	20	21
22	23	24	25	26	27	28
29	30					

October
Mo	Tu	We	Th	Fr	Sa	Su
	1	2	3	4	5	
6	7	8	9	10	11	12
13	14	15	16	17	18	19
20	21	22	23	24	25	26
27	28	29	30	31		

November
Mo	Tu	We	Th	Fr	Sa	Su
					1	2
3	4	5	6	7	8	9
10	11	12	13	14	15	16
17	18	19	20	21	22	23
24	25	26	27	28	29	30

December
Mo	Tu	We	Th	Fr	Sa	Su
1	2	3	4	5	6	7
8	9	10	11	12	13	14
15	16	17	18	19	20	21
22	23	24	25	26	27	28
29	30	31				

Maybe you could highlight difficult times

Special days can be hard

List days that you feel will be harder than others and suggest ways to cope with them.

Birthdays

Happy Birthday "   "
It's sure to be the best one yet,
Though you left us here behind.
Did you think that we'd forget?

Your cake this year, will surely be,
A beauty to behold.
With the icing made of Silver,
And the candles made of Gold.

Yes, your birthday in Heaven,
Will be such a grand affair.
And I know you'll look so lovely,
With a halo in your hair.

The Angels will come from everywhere,
To sing your birthday song.
And I know they'll be so happy,
That you've joined, God's Happy Throng.

No I can't send a card this year,
Or give a gift so fine.
So I'll just send a special prayer,
To that wonderful _____ of mine

How I will celebrate our Birthdays

A Special Day for Me

Valentine's Day –
Fill this page with love

Easter

The Easter story

How does this make me feel?

How will my Easter be different?

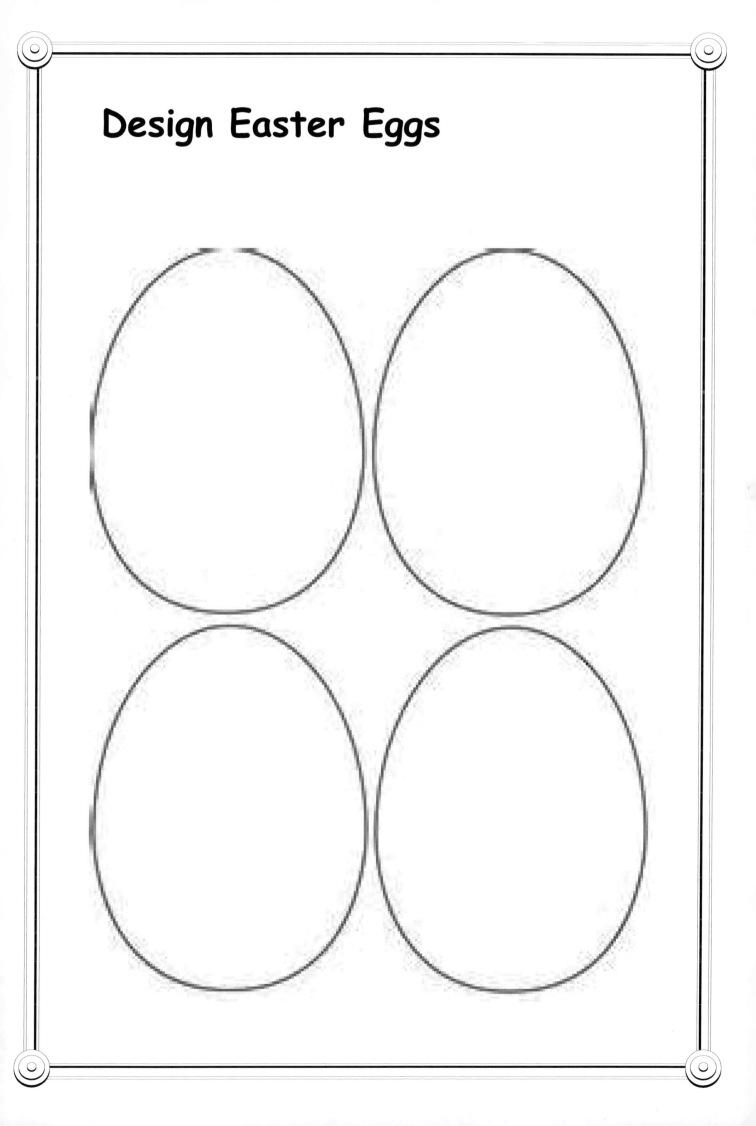

Mother's Day

Father's Day

Christmas

Santa, are you listening?
I need a little time.
I can't write my Christmas wish,
Without this _____ of mine.

Santa, I don't want presents,
Or lots of fuss, and chat.
Please Santa, all I want
Is my darling _____ back.

Santa, you can't make miracles,
Or turn back the hands of time.
All I have Santa, is one wish,
That's to see that _____ of mine

Santa, take me a letter,
Across the rainbow up above,
That's my only wish Santa,
To my Darling _____ above.

Santa, tell _____, we love _____
Give _____ everything you've got.
Please Santa, help me please.
It's not asking you a lot.

Santa, that's my Christmas wish.
Will you do it just for me?
Send my love, and all I have.
For my lovely _____ to see.

New Year's Eve & Day

This is how I remember you

These are my plans for the future